# Light and Colour

## John Stringer

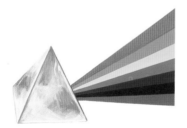

## Contents

# A world without light

Can you imagine a world
without light? It's a hard thing
to do. Think how you feel in a
power cut, or in your bedroom
at night, or in a dark corner
when you're hiding from
your friends.

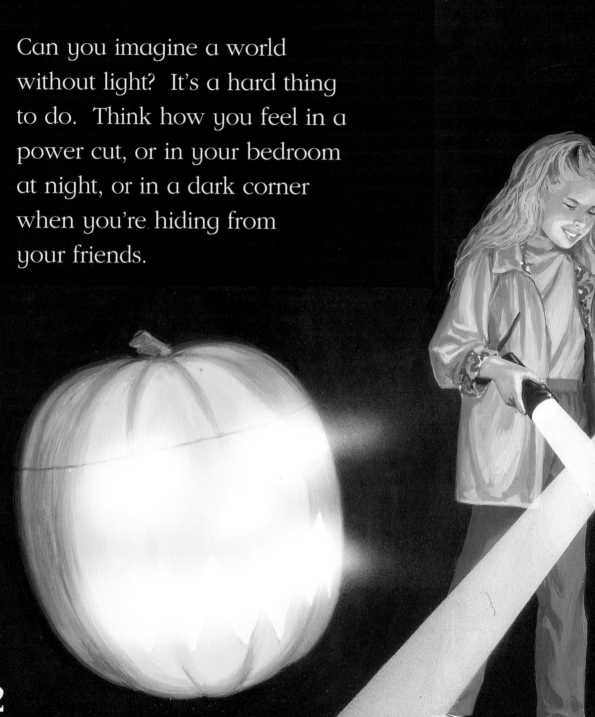

## Chasing away the dark

Most of us don't like darkness for too long. In fact, ever since people first lived in caves, they've liked to chase away the darkness with a light.

# Where does light come from?

Think of the different kinds of light there are.

## Sunlight

Every morning we see the Sun's light – the light we use in the daytime. By evening the sun's light grows dim, and it's hard to see.

## Electric light

At dusk, electric lights light up our homes, and make us feel cosy. Outside, street lights, signs, and shop windows are all bright with electric lights.

## Firelight

It could be a candle or a bonfire. Any burning flame will give a flickering light. And it's hot, too!

# The burning Sun

The Sun is a burning ball of fire
which gives us heat and
light.  Without it, the
Earth would be
cold and
dark.

### Does the Sun shine at night?
The Sun shines in space all night
long.  We can't see it then because
of the way the Earth turns.  Shine a
torch on a globe to see how one
side is light when the other is dark.

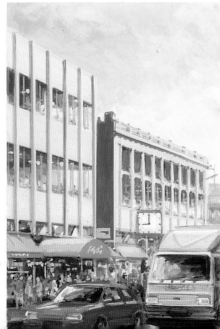

## Through the day

As the Sun rises in the sky, more heat and light reach us. As it goes down in the evening, we get less heat and less light.

## Blinding light

Never look straight at the Sun – even through sunglasses. Its light is so bright that it could damage your eyes.

# Sunshine through space

## On Earth

On a sunny day, the Sun's rays stream down, casting strong dark shadows. But even on a grey day, the Sun's rays are strong enough to light a room.

## On the Moon

The Sun's rays light up the Moon, too.
The first people on the Moon stood in the
Sun's light, throwing strong black shadows on
the dusty ground.

Without the Sun's light, the Moon would be
totally dark.  We wouldn't be able to see it.

# Electric lights

Before electricity, people used candles and oil and gas lamps to see in the dark. These lights weren't very bright and could easily start a fire.

## Light from a bulb

Today, at the flick of a switch, electricity flows through wires into a light bulb, giving us a bright, safe and steady light.

## Torchlight

Torches are useful because they run on batteries. Batteries are like small parcels of electricity that can be moved from place to place. They are very safe, but they don't last for ever.

# Shadows

Rays of light can shine through windows because they are made of glass, and glass is clear. But rays of light can't shine through something solid like a wall. That's when shadows appear.

## You have a shadow

Your body is solid, and makes a shadow where rays of light cannot go. Your shadow follows you everywhere on a sunny day, and copies everything you do.

12

## Shadows on the wall

It's not just sunlight that makes shadows. Try using a torch to make shadows on the wall.

# Seeing with light

No one can see in the dark. You can only see the things around you if light is shining on them. As rays of light fall on these things, they bounce the light back. This is called reflection. Many of the things you see in these pictures do not give off light themselves. They reflect it from somewhere else.

## Light in your eyes

What kind of light are you using to read this book? Its rays are being reflected from the book into your eyes.

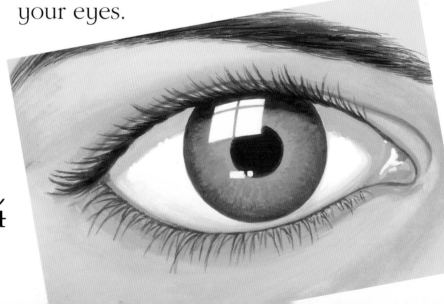

# The eyes of a cat

Cats hunt at night. They can see in the dark.

16

## Open wide

Inside a cat's eye there is a part which is rather like a window. When it opens very wide, it collect lots of light – even when it seems dark to us.

## Shiny eyes

Have you noticed how a cat's eyes shine in the dark? At the back of their eyes is a shiny layer, like a mirror. It reflects most of the light the eyes have collected.

What other animals can see in the dark?

17

# Mirrors

Look in a mirror and what do you see?
Yourself, of course.

## Why do you see yourself?

All the things you see around you reflect the light.
But a mirror does it better than anything else
because it has such a smooth and shiny surface.
When you look in a mirror, the rays of light bounce
straight back, making a very sharp picture of
yourself. We call this picture an image.

## Mirrors in nature

Ponds and lakes have
shiny surfaces, too.
They often
reflect trees
and clouds.

# Funny mirrors

Have you ever seen yourself in a Hall of Mirrors? You often find these funny mirrors at fairs. They make you look hugely fat, as thin as a pencil, or very bendy.

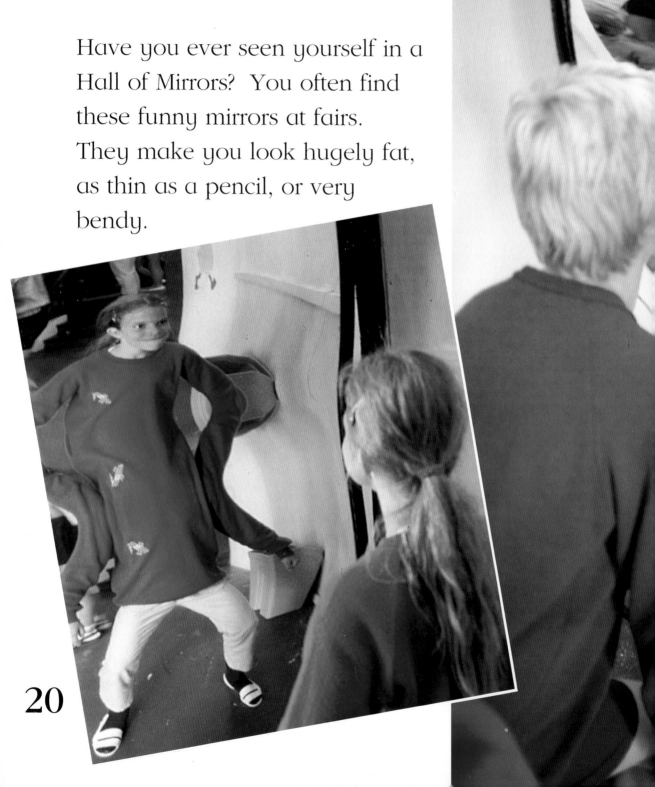

## How do they work?

Fairground mirrors don't have a flat surface like the mirrors you have at home. They bulge in and out. When rays of light hit the curvy surface, they can't bounce back in a straight line. This is why they reflect such a strange image.

The same thing happens when you look at yourself in a spoon.

21

# Using reflection

A smooth shiny surface reflects light well. People have thought up clever ways to use reflectors.

## On your bike

Cycling at night can be dangerous because car drivers can't always see you. Bicycle reflectors are shiny bits of plastic that reflect a car's headlights back to the driver. Car drivers see the reflection – and they see the bike.

## On the road

Dark roads can be dangerous for drivers, too. Special reflectors in the middle of a road reflect a car's bright headlights. They help drivers to see

 the road ahead.

22

# The colour of light

Sunlight looks white, but it's actually made up of many different colours. You only see these colours when the light is split up.

Prism

## Rainbow colours

During a spring shower, sunlight will sometimes shine through the rain. The drops of rain split up the white light into its different colours – and this makes a beautiful rainbow.

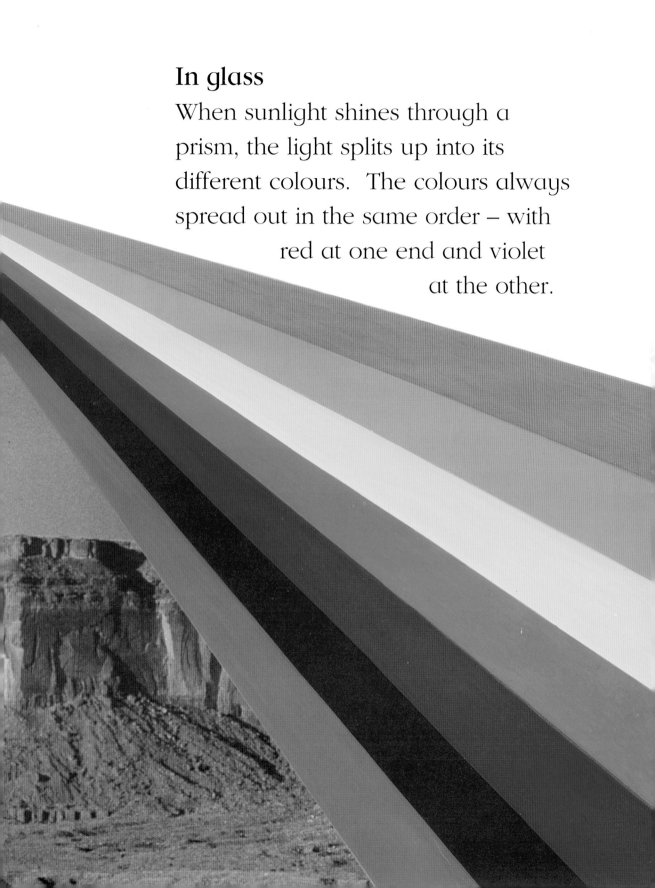

## In glass

When sunlight shines through a prism, the light splits up into its different colours. The colours always spread out in the same order – with red at one end and violet at the other.

# Hundreds of colours

Shops sell tins of paint in every colour under the sun. Yet most of them are mixed from just three colours – yellow, blue and red.

## Mixing colours

Mixing red with yellow makes orange. Mixing blue with yellow makes green. Mixing paints in different ways gives dozens of new colours.

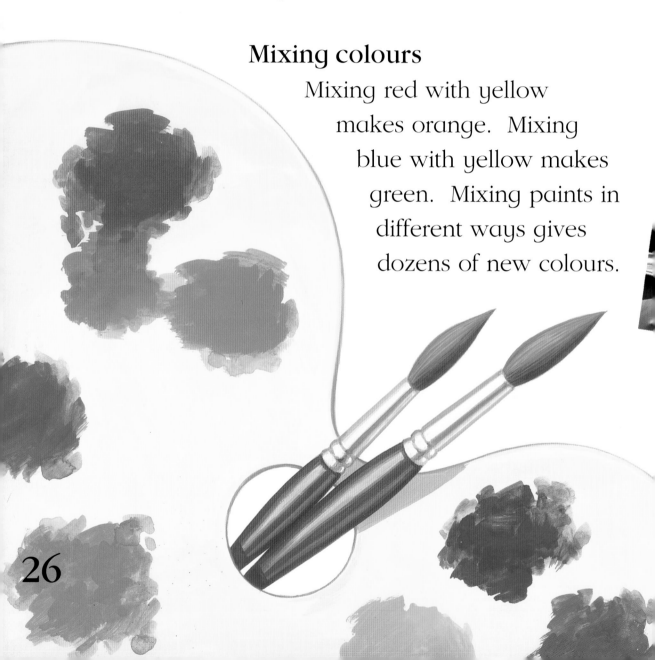

## Shades of colour

Adding black to a colour makes it
darker. Adding white makes it lighter.
Each colour can come in many different
shades. Think of all the shades there
are of the colour blue.

# Colours in nature

## Colours warn

Bright colours sometimes act as a warning to animals. The poison arrow frog is bright orange and black. Its colours tell other animals that it's very unpleasant to eat. The wasp's yellow and black stripes warn others of its sting.

## Colours hide

Some animals have colours that
blend in with their surroundings.
This makes them harder to see.
The Arctic hare is white against
the winter snow. With luck, a
hungry fox may not see it.

# Using colour

Some colours are bright and exciting.
Others are calm and restful. We like to
wear different colours at different times.

## Danger!

On the roads, strong colours and flashing lights are used to give warnings. They stand out brightly on dull, foggy days. A red traffic light means stop. A blue light flashing on a police car, fire engine or ambulance means it's rushing to an emergency.

## At rest

Soft colours are more restful. People often use them to decorate their homes.

What kind of colours do you like?

# Index

HarperCollins Children's Books
A Division of HarperCollins Publishers Ltd, 77–85 Fulham Palace Road, Hammersmith, London W6 8JB
First published 1994 in the United Kingdom
Copyright © HarperCollins*Publishers* 1994
Prepared by *specialist publishing services* 090 857 307

ISBN 0 00 196545 X
A CIP record is available from the British Library

Illustrated by Mike Lacey
Photographs by Desmond Burden/TSW: p16; Caroline Field/Life File: p5; Barbara Filet/TSW: p24;
Michael Fogden/OSF: p28; Geoscience: p4; David Hiser/TSW: p11; Michael Leach/OSF: p28;
Brock May/OSF: p29; Terry O'Brian/Life File: p31; Rex Features: pp21/22;
Andrew Tyndall/Life File: pp8, 18; TSW: pp5, 9, 31; Ken Whitmore/TSW: p27.
Series editor: Nick Hutchins; Editing: Claire Llewellyn; Design: Eric Drewery/Susi Martin;
Picture research: Lorraine Sennett
Printed and bound in Hong Kong